Kiff Slemmons

Re:Pair & Imperfection

Copyright © 2006
By the City of Chicago
Department of Cultural Affairs
78 East Washington Street
Chicago, IL 60602

All rights reserved

ISBN 0-938903-37-3

Published in the United States of America by the City of Chicago Department of Cultural Affairs in conjunction with the exhibition *Re:Pair & Imperfection* held from March 25, 2006 – May 28, 2006 in the Michigan Avenue Galleries of the Chicago Cultural Center.

Layout+Typography
the JNL graphic design

Printing
Original Smith

Photography
Rod Slemmons

Organized by the Chicago Department of Cultural Affairs, exhibitions and related educational programming presented by DCA at the Chicago Cultural Center are partially supported by a grant from the Illinois Arts Council, a state agency. The Michigan Avenue Galleries are supported by CHASE. This exhibition and catalog received additional support from the Rotasa Foundation.

City of Chicago
Richard M. Daley, Mayor

Chicago Department of Cultural Affairs
Lois Weisberg, Commissioner

Gregory G. Knight
Deputy Commissioner/Visual Arts

Lanny Silverman
Curator of Exhibitions

Sofia Zutautas
Assistant Curator of Exhibitions

Greg Lunceford
Exhibition Designer/Installation Coordinator

**chicago cultural center**

78 East Washington Street
77 East Randolph Street
Chicago, IL 60602
312-744-6630
www.chicagoculturalcenter.org

Kiff Slemmons   Re:Pair
& Imperfection

25 March – 28 May 2006

The Chicago Cultural Center 78 East Washington Chicago IL 60603

Sandra Enterline

▶ Kiff Slemmons
**Replica** and **Pouch**
Replica: pin, 3 diameter × ¼
Pouch: pendant, 2½ diameter × ¼
Replica: Silver
Pouch: Silver and stingray skin

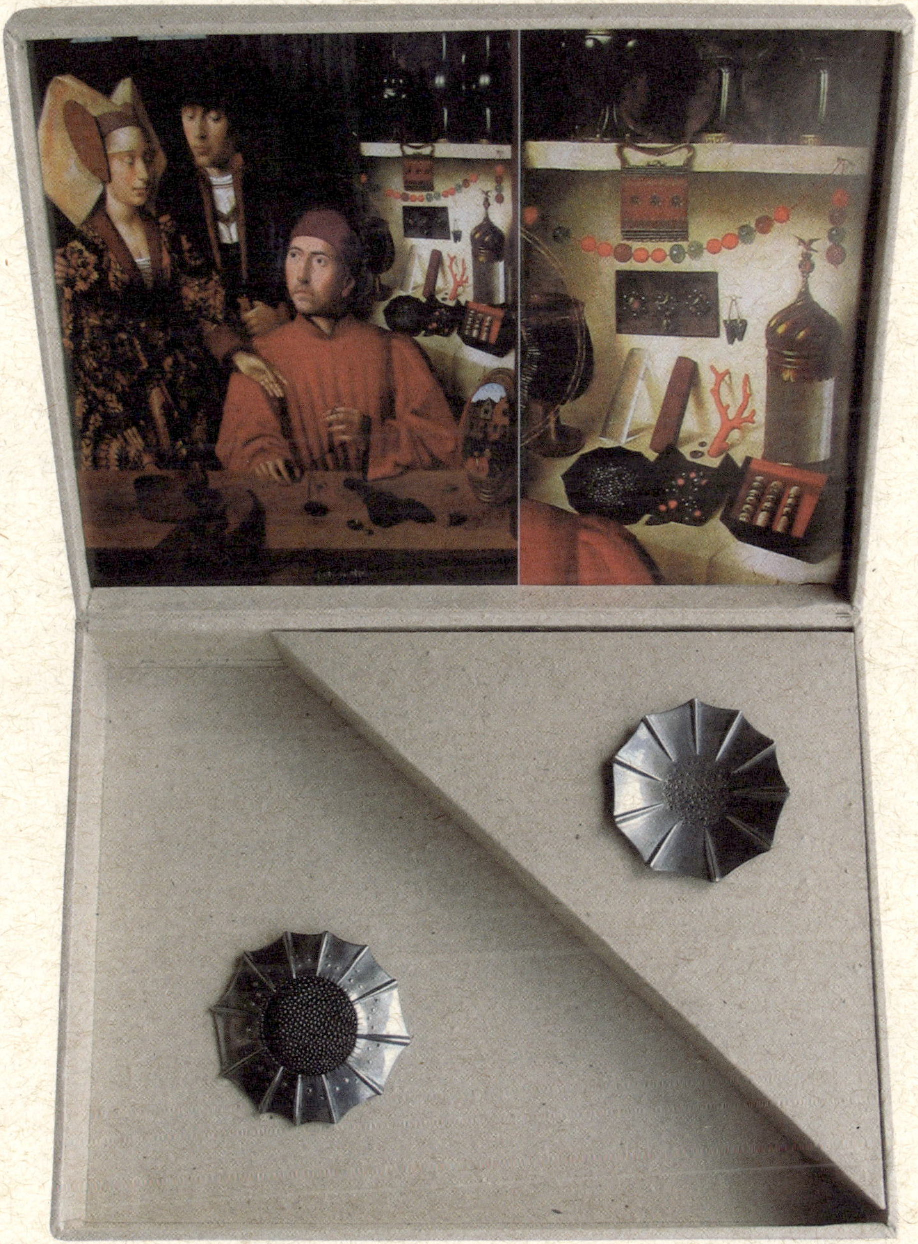

**Foreword & Acknowledgements**

Lanny Silverman, Curator of Exhibitions, Chicago Department of Cultural Affairs

In my awkward attempts to try to summarize Kiff Slemmons' work to others, I have found myself using the term "conceptual jeweler," which really doesn't do justice to the complexity of her endeavors. What is important to note is that this project actually manages to transcend the usual art world squabbles over jewelry as craft vs. art. While Slemmons creates beautiful objects, they are beautiful objects that call into question our very notions of beauty and perfection. By incorporating disparate found materials and discards from other artists, this exhibition leads us to reexamine the notion of a mistake, as well as elevating refuse, the humble cast-off, and even decay into the conversation about beauty.

The notion of imperfection is a rich one. In her exceptionally well-thought-out exhibition proposal, Slemmons brought up the telling example of conservators' attempts to "restore" Glenn Gould's beloved piano to customary standards. Considering that he spent a lifetime modifying it in an attempt to make it adhere to his quixotic sense of perfection/imperfection, this is more than ironic. (To add to this irony, Gould was the master of beautiful phrasing of Bach, yet he often hummed quite imperfectly along with his playing in an attempt to mouth the perfect phrasing, which he felt his piano playing couldn't ever achieve.) When Slemmons completes other artists' cast-offs and mistakes, she does so with considerable sensitivity to the artists' intentions, all the while demonstrating the relativity of such concepts as intentionality and mistake. This has important ramifications for jewelers and metalsmiths, working as they do in a field in which obsessive craft often pervades. It has broader implications as well, reminding us that not only can we learn from so-called mistakes but we can create from them in what is a continuous and creative process of examination and reevaluation.

Slemmons' work also calls into question notions of style and individuality in a complex manner. By attempting to understand and complete these fragments she has put herself in a relationship with the various artists and their styles. Slemmons' strategy is not to adopt a fixed style but rather to adapt to the specific problem set before her, always in relationship to others. This is an unusual and fascinating approach, especially given our cultural preoccupation with individuality, most pronounced in the art world.

This work engages the viewer with just such a rich set of questions about art as well as life, and in a manner that is endlessly rewarding. While questioning beauty and the act of creation, it manages to engage and delight us with its very beauty and creativity.

Foremost, I would like to thank Kiff Slemmons for her extraordinary amount of thought, work and passion in this endeavor. Thanks go as well to all the artists who lent their fragments and their completed works to make this project possible. This exhibition was the result of a collaboration with representatives of the Society of North American Goldsmiths (S.N.A.G.), whose annual conference is being held in Chicago in 2006. *Re:Pair and Imperfection* was proposed as an exhibition to be held concurrently with the conference. I would like to thank S.N.A.G. for their assistance. Special thanks go to Carla Reiter whose tireless efforts as project coordinator and editor were essential to the realization of this project. Particular gratitude is owed to Susan Cummins and the Rotasa Foundation. The scope of this project and especially this catalog would not have been possible without its generous support. Thanks are also extended to Rod Slemmons for his photography, to Kim Kopp and Karin Vance for their fabrication of the lovely boxes that house elements of the exhibition, and to Arte Papel in

Oaxaca, Mexico for the handmade paper that covers the boxes. Our gratitude is also extended to Tacey Rosolowski for her thoughtful essay and to Jason Pickleman of the JNL Graphic Design for his beautiful catalog design and to Original Smith for their careful printing of this publication.

As always, I'd like to acknowledge the continuing support and guidance of the Department of Cultural Affairs Exhibition Advisory Committee, and to thank DCA Commissioner Lois Weisberg and other DCA colleagues, especially in the Visual Arts Division—Gregory Knight, Asst. Deputy Commissioner/Visual Arts, Greg Lunceford, Exhibition Designer/Installation Coordinator and Sofia Zutautas, Exhibition Coordinator/Assistant Curator.

# From Fragment to Connection

### Tacey A. Rosolowski, Ph.D

OVER THE PAST THIRTY YEARS Kiff Slemmons has made a name creating jewelry as rich in concept and meaning as it is varied in form and material. Viewers familiar with two previous projects, *Hands of the Heroes* (fifty pieces) and *Insectopedia* (twenty-six pieces), may already be aware that Slemmons uses the series to organize her creative process and produce work with the greatest possible nuance. Through a linked set of objects Slemmons explores a focal concept, unfolding its many complexities through direct and repeated engagement with materials and technique. The current exhibition, *Re:Pair and Imperfection*, is exemplary from this perspective. It invites the viewer to watch an artist bring artistic fascinations developed over a long career to an entirely new level.

    Slemmons began the project by writing to artists (largely jewelers and metalsmiths) to request a piece of work that they had abandoned because it was damaged or no longer of interest. She made it clear that she would create objects of jewelry from each artist's 'fragments' (her term for the contributions), though she also stated that she did not intend to fix or complete them. Rather than repairing the fragments in any conventional sense, she would use them as an occasion to link her own aesthetic with that of each contributing artist. The objects created for *Re:Pair and Imperfection* are unexpected hybrids, the result of Slemmons' exploratory "pairing" and "re-pairing" of aesthetics. Centrally concerned with the nature of relationships, the exhibition raises issues of significance for all artists working in today's pan-national and pan-cultural art scene, with implications that resonate beyond the confines of art.

    Slemmons' concern with the concept of repair began thirty years ago, when she restored a collection of ethnic jewelry and sensed her responsibility to unknown artists with cultural and artistic sensibilities distant from her own. This nuanced idea took on deeper significance in 2003, when U.S. troops invaded Iraq. Slemmons saw the U.S. reject diplomacy and impose its political, economic and cultural will on other nations. She was dismayed at the destruction of a cultural and artistic heritage going back to the beginnings of civilization. Vietnam inevitably came to mind: in both Vietnam and Iraq, she says, "We destroy a country and then repair it in our own way."

Language is often key as Slemmons reframes conceptual issues from outside the realm of art in terms that can be approached artistically. The Iraq invasion catalyzed Slemmons' thinking and set the conceptual stakes of the exhibition: *Re:Pair and Imperfection* is, fundamentally, concerned with parameters of correct conduct—in short, with ethics. Slemmons re-envisioned "repair" as an arena for establishing relationships, one in which she could explore productive alternatives to dominance and aggression. Before beginning work with the fragments, Slemmons stated her imperatives: with each fragment she would explore how to "take from without taking over," how "to add to something without interfering with it"; "I never wanted to impose myself on the fragments," she affirmed, nor "offend the fragments' integrity."

Eighteen well-known artists such as Otto Künzli, Joe Wood, Lisa Gralnick, Gary Griffin, and Myra Mimlitsch-Gray contributed thirty fragments. Slemmons has created twenty-nine works, each displayed in its own box. A black and white photo of the fragment in its original form hangs above Slemmons' work, and finished objects by the contributing artists are also displayed. With these references, the viewer can trace how Slemmons relates her pieces to the contributors' styles.

One measure of these relationships arises from her handling of the fragments' "imperfections." In some cases Slemmons used the damage; in others she trimmed it away; at times no flaws were evident. "Imperfection" is a slippery designation—and an aesthetic concept for Slemmons. A perfectly executed vessel or jewelry object can fail to engage her interest and she points to the Japanese concept of *wabi-sabi* to define the qualities that intrigue her and that she strives for in her own work: roughness, serendipity, asymmetry, natural surfaces and unexpected conjunctions of materials. Slemmons also uses "imperfection" to refer to such features, an advantageous designation for the second theme of this exhibition. The term invokes a tension of opposites (perfection vs. a falling away from a pristine state). Slemmons worked just such a line of tension as she explored how each artist's "imperfection" might be recuperated (a vehicle of re:pairing) within a different aesthetic.

Her artistic persona undergoes the most striking transformation under the influence of Sandra Enterline's fragment, a rough-surfaced silver hemisphere with decorative apertures in the center. The fragment brought to mind a Petrus Christus painting, *A Goldsmith in His Shop* (a lateral gesture characteristic of Slemmons' thinking): on the bench behind the goldsmith (who may represent Saint Elegius, the patron saint of jewelers) lies an open jeweler's pouch, glittering with gems. Slemmons keyed on this object when she began to work with the fragment, adding a partner piece to create a play on positive and negative shapes. The resulting brooches are symmetrical, highly polished, with delicately refined details.

"Minimalism and perfection make Sandra's work effective," Slemmons says. She could find no recognizable imperfections in Enterline's fragment which, she notes, "drew me to a perfection beyond my usual approach." Like a chameleon, Slemmons has assimilated to the artist's style, though the contours of her own aesthetic show through: she oxidized the brooches, embellished one with a piece of dyed and polished stingray skin; and she displays the pair with the Christus image [PAGE 5] to invoke the tradition of craftsmanship that Enterline exemplifies today.

Slemmons wanted to examine such self-transformation in minute detail. The fact that she has willingly undergone this shift with each object and contributor in the exhibition shows unusual courage. It also demonstrates how thoroughly Slemmons melds concept and practice in her projects. She understands the postmodern given that all artists work in a tradition and borrow from history, from one another and from a culturally-shared language of visual images. Moreover, she has created an arena in which the viewer can see how this fact of artistic existence shapes living creative practice. Slemmons offers a practical critique of the art world's cult of individuality: the artist is an autonomous and unified ego that determines its own creative path and imposes its will on materials. Slemmons engages a different part of her artistic ego—one fixed in a network of influences and more fungible than boundaried in its receptiveness. "I'm discovering," Slemmons says, "that all of these people are in my work."

Within this universe of connections, Slemmons strikes a different balance with each contributor's fragment. Enamelist June Schwarcz sent a vessel with collapsed sides. Slemmons trimmed out a strip of its fiery oranges and yellows and mounted it in an ebony rectangle. The result is a gorgeous object, a formal portrait of primary elements: the enamelist's fire, and the charcoal used by jewelers in heating and soldering metal [PAGE 57]. Joyce Scott offered beaded fragments and Slemmons wove a female figure, a hand and a "fire tongue" into a narrative of self-transformation: an African woman is on a ship bound for the New World and she speaks, through the "fire tongue," to a silhouette (her future self) on the destination's shore. The neckpiece underscores the artists' commonalities [PAGE 61]. What Scott might make in beads, Slemmons creates in street-textured metal; a narrative Scott personalizes in figures, Slemmons might approach conceptually. Differences emerged with Joe Wood's silver armature. The fragment reminded Slemmons of a bridge and she emphasized its rough unfinished surfaces, adding a beat-up miniature car (a found object) that speeds across the structure into an eerie shadow cast by a crow soaring overhead [PAGE 73]. *Bridge* builds a narrative snapshot from constructivist minimalism and poses a question: Who is leading whom in this bridging of aesthetics?

Slemmons has always questioned individual ownership of art, believing that "it takes many people to own a piece." Throughout her career she has acted on this by refusing to sign her work. In this exhibition she goes further and replicates the space of open exchange in which any art-making takes place. With each fragment Slemmons explores a distinct mode of "taking from without taking over" and the following questions must be asked anew: What is the artistic status of these hybrid pieces? Who exactly has made them? To whom do they belong? They are not collaborations, since Slemmons solicited no input; but with each fragment she nonetheless sets up an interactive relationship with another public persona. The term "dialogized work" (a term from literary critic, M.M. Bakhtin) characterizes the achievement of these pieces. In dialogue a speaker wants to be understood and shapes phrases *for* someone, so the language contains an impression of the listener. A dialogized work includes different styles or perspectives presented so they respond to one another.

*Argilos* is a particularly vivid illustration [PAGE 27] Thomas Gentille contributed a chipped synthetic resin disk carved as a geometrical study of a circle housed in a square. This was the most formal of the fragments, and Slemmons continued to carve in this spirit. She eliminated the chip and most of the curved portions, revealing a Gentillian clarity of line. Then she placed a disk of industrial-grade ceramic in the brooch's center—hence the title. "Argilos" is derived from "argil," a chalky white potter's clay. The addition strengthens Gentille's formal geometry while revealing Slemmons' admitted "latent formalism"—though with a found object characteristic of her own approach. Slemmons also re-placed the formica segments from the chipped edge (cut into triangles). The line where Gentille's form splinters into a random intersection of planes marks a place where formalism erupts into *wabi-sabi*. It also stages a dialogue through imperfection: Slemmons literally transforms Gentille's damage so that self-contained formalism might re-emerge as aesthetic chaos. The movement between the two aesthetics creates a third not fully encompassed by either.

Western artists have been slow to act on the knowledge that art is not an extension of a single ego, but is made (and consumed) in a broad human context. Slemmons has given herself over to demonstrating this fact. Rarely does an exhibition provide such an intimate glimpse of an artist's manner of working, or guide the exhibition viewer so carefully from material engagement with objects to their theoretical implications. Slemmons offers her viewers a unique opportunity to experience the array of relationships that feed artistic creativity and production. She has celebrated her bonds with her contributors. She invites her viewers to join her. ✽

## Letter from Kiff Slemmons
## to colleagues concerning *Re:Pair and Imperfection*, 2004

Lately I have been thinking of the idea of perfection in craft and at the same time of the importance of imperfection in art in general. Craft is often characterized by the refinement of technique and form. In earlier definitions of craft the form served the function, and design was considered successful if it had most perfectly accomplished this purpose. And in this process beauty also could be produced. The antiquated idea of quality, however, firmly depended on perfect execution and the absence of flaws. But we have all seen, and even produced, amazingly hand crafted things that still lack vitality. What is missing?

Maybe one way to understand this missing something is to consider examining imperfection and what it means. When I try to define the value of imperfection, I often think of work that has a certain presence (character, or even ambiguity), and that presence may be enhanced by signs of the hand, evidence of the maker (or process marks). Sometimes if an object is too perfect, it feels closed and paralyzed— it doesn't invite further engagement. It can't sustain attention. This, of course, isn't always true. Exceptions would be really fine minimal work, or the exquisite simplicity and refinement of much of Japanese functional craft. But on the other hand, Japanese potters make purposefully awkward tea ceremony bowls that specifically address the idea of imperfection, inviting the holders to complete the form, or further, to imagine a perfect form for themselves.

Trying to articulate this importance of imperfections is difficult, so as usual I'm trying to surround the idea with already made examples for support and insight. Examples that come from different cultures at different times help to elucidate the contemporary manifestations of this issue, and also help me imbue my own work with this quality. For someone who has perfectionist tendencies it is not necessarily easy to trust imperfection. One aspect of trying to understand flaws is to look at both the physical and philosophical aspects of repair. In our throwaway culture, repair is not necessarily highly regarded as a means of solving problems. Better to throw away than to fix. But more is thrown away than meets the eye. What is also lost is what can be learned from trying to fix something, and the satisfaction of rendering it useable or refreshing it in some way.

When I first started making jewelry I spent some time repairing old ethnic pieces from a private collection. I realize now that this activity was really my education in design, composition, fabrication, and engineering. I so admired the work of the anonymous jewelers that I wanted to preserve the integrity of the pieces as much as possible even when whole sections were missing. At that time, I wouldn't presume that I could enhance or rejuvenate the old pieces by my own sense of design. A year ago I was looking at this same collection and admired the repair on an African ivory cuff. I was surprised to learn and then remember that I had done it 30 years before. It made me feel good that I had invented a repair that was obviously not "authentic" but the spirit of the piece was still very much intact. The elusive vitality that we all keep looking for was there. This was a very modest endeavor, a minor detail, but I've been thinking of it again as a way to investigate imperfection. How far can you go and still maintain the integrity of a piece? Often we might think obvious repair makes an object more interesting rather than causing us to lament the damage. The Japanese certainly understand this when repairing a special tea bowl. The cracks are not only left showing but are accentuated with gold leaf.

These ideas seem to me to have application in the larger contemporary geopolitical picture. Our international policy seems to be more geared toward throwing away in the form of destroying and starting over, rather than painstaking repair—rather than trying to understand problems in depth as a potential solution. My generation still remembers the Viet Nam era military phrase: "It became necessary to destroy the village in order to liberate it." Which really meant, "rather than having to figure it out."

I would like to explore several of these ideas (big ones and little ones) simultaneously and come up with some metaphoric conclusions. Not by talking or theorizing, but by doing what we do best—making jewelry. Imagine! First of all there is the fast becoming obsolete idea of repair, including its history of either convincing restoration or acknowledgement of acceptable imperfection—and I mean this in both the larger political sense and the smaller mechanical sense. Second, there is that stalled out idea sitting on the back of the worktable waiting for, literally, revision. And third, there is the notion of intentional imperfection, to give the gods of creation, who have big egos, the opportunity to win.

Here is a curious and strange proposal. Would you be willing to give me a broken, incomplete or inconclusive fragment of yours (a fragment with part of its "character" showing, one that is conceptually part way) that is sitting around doing nothing at present? I would set out to "fix it", which could involve many possibilities but would end up in a finished piece of jewelry. I am not necessarily suggesting collaboration, though in a sense it would become that. If you prefer, I would not say that it came from you. However, I like the idea of naming the piece after you in some encoded way. Needless to say, I wouldn't even be asking if I didn't respect and celebrate your work. I also wouldn't be asking if I didn't have similar things sitting around on my own table.

I would take these fragments and try to complete them in some way, though it's not possible to make them perfect. Or, alternatively, I would finish them as an homage to imperfection. It might also be interesting to you to see how I see where they might have been going for you before they got stuck, or broken, or boring. In any case, I would hope to expand and celebrate their orphaned vitality into a finished work that would still acknowledge the qualifications and difficulties of repair, conclusion, and perfection. But I would not guarantee success.

Even if you think this is a crazy idea, I'd appreciate your thoughts. If you don't think it is crazy, send me a package. I would like to see what is possible and perhaps there would be material for an exhibition (or for an essay). My real purpose here is exploratory, as I guess you probably understand.

—Kiff Slemmons

## Contributing Artists

**Bettina Dittlman**, *Egglham, Germany*
**Sandra Enterline**, *San Francisco, California*
**Thomas Gentille**, *New York, New York*
**Lisa Gralnick**, *Madison, Wisconsin*
**Gary Griffin**, *Bloomfield Hills, Michigan*
**Daniel Jocz**, *Cambridge, Massachusetts*
**Esther Knobel**, *Jerusalem, Israel*
**Keith Lewis**, *Seattle, Washington*
**Otto Künzli**, *Munich, Germany*
**Bruce Metcalf**, *Bala Cynwyd, Pennsylvania*
**Myra Mimlitsch-Gray**, *Stone Ridge, New York*
**June Schwarcz**, *Sausalito, California*
**Joyce Scott**, *Baltimore, Maryland*
**Ramona Solberg**, *Seattle, Washington*
**Rachelle Thiewes**, *El Paso, Texas*
**Terry Turrell**, *Seattle, Washington*
**J. Fred Woell**, *Deer Isle, Maine*
**Joe Wood**, *Cambridge, Massachusetts*

# Plates

Bettina Dittlman

Kiff Slemmons
**Aranea**
Pin: 3 × 8 × 1 ¾
Silver, enameled copper

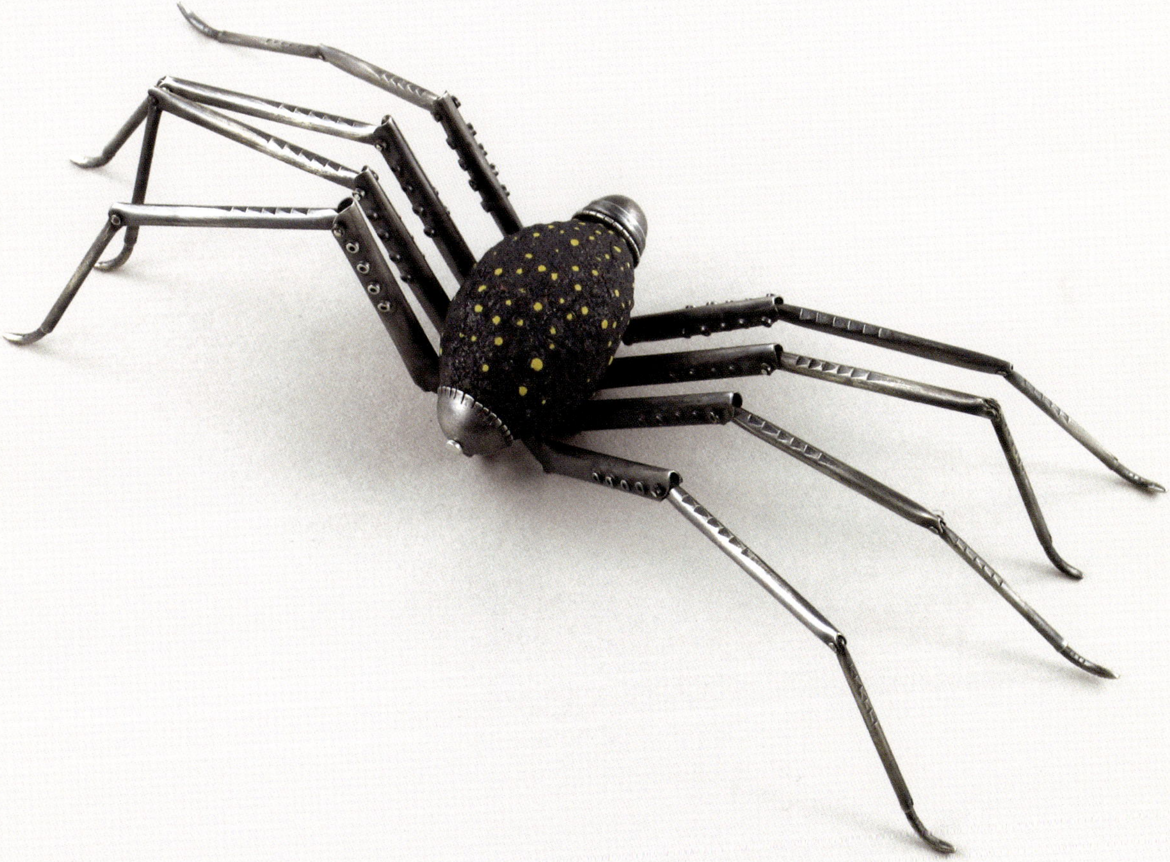

Sandra Enterline

Kiff Slemmons
**Whisker Squints**
Goggles: 1¾ × 7 × 3
Silver, pearl, cat whiskers

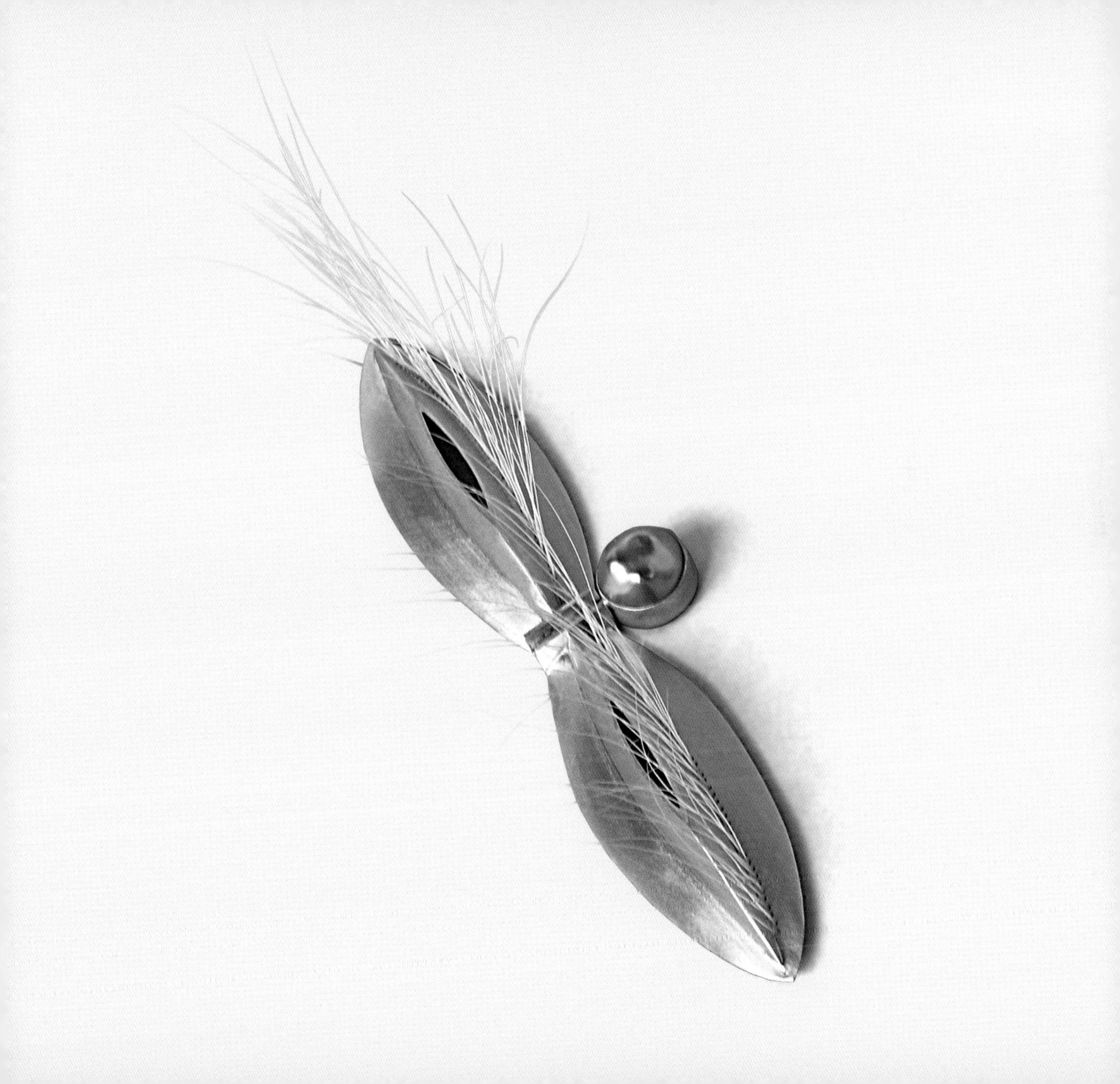

▶

Thomas Gentille

Kiff Slemmons
**Argilos**
Pin: 3 × 2 ¼ × ½
Synthetic resin, porcelain

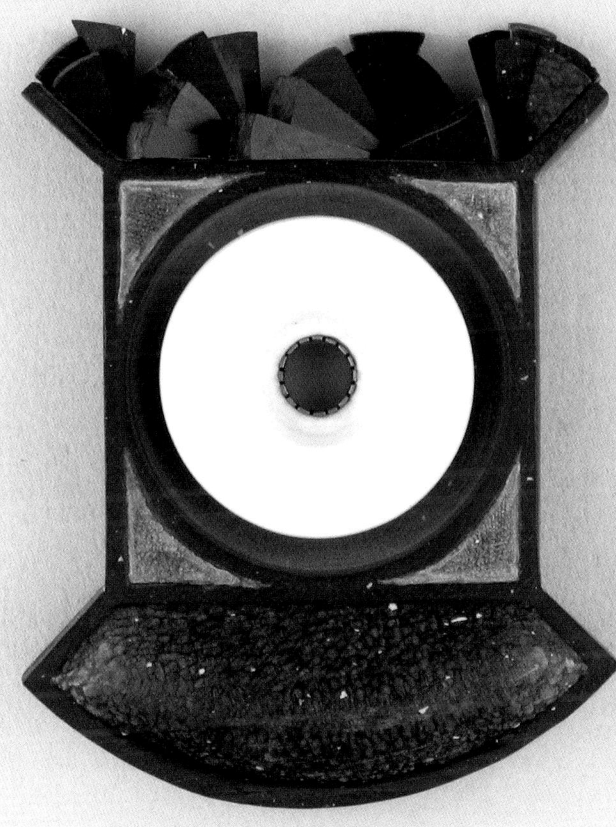

Thomas Gentille

Kiff Slemmons
**Gift**
Pin: 3 ¼ × 2 ½ × ¼
Silver, fused gold, titanium

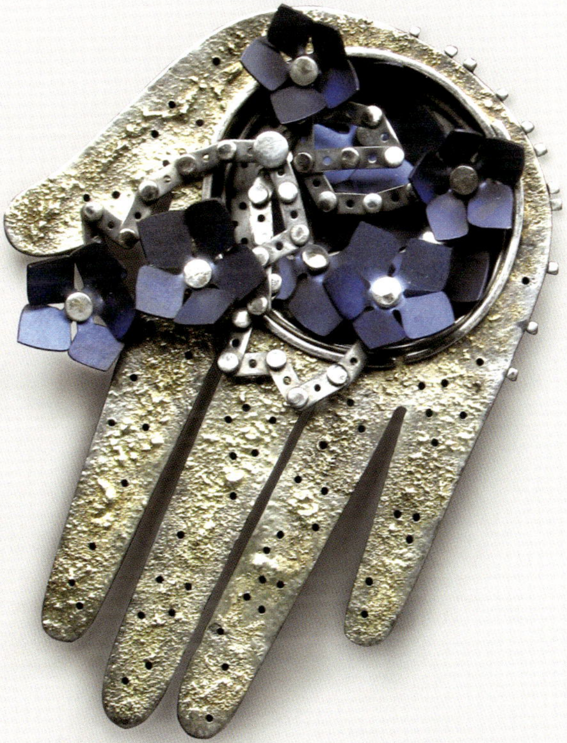

Thomas Gentille

Kiff Slemmons
**Relic**
Two Finger Ring: 1 × 1 ¾ × 1 ¼
Silver, mica, wrapped synthetic resin chip


Kiff Slemmons
**Fault**
Two Finger Ring: 1 × 1 ¾ × 1 ¼
Silver

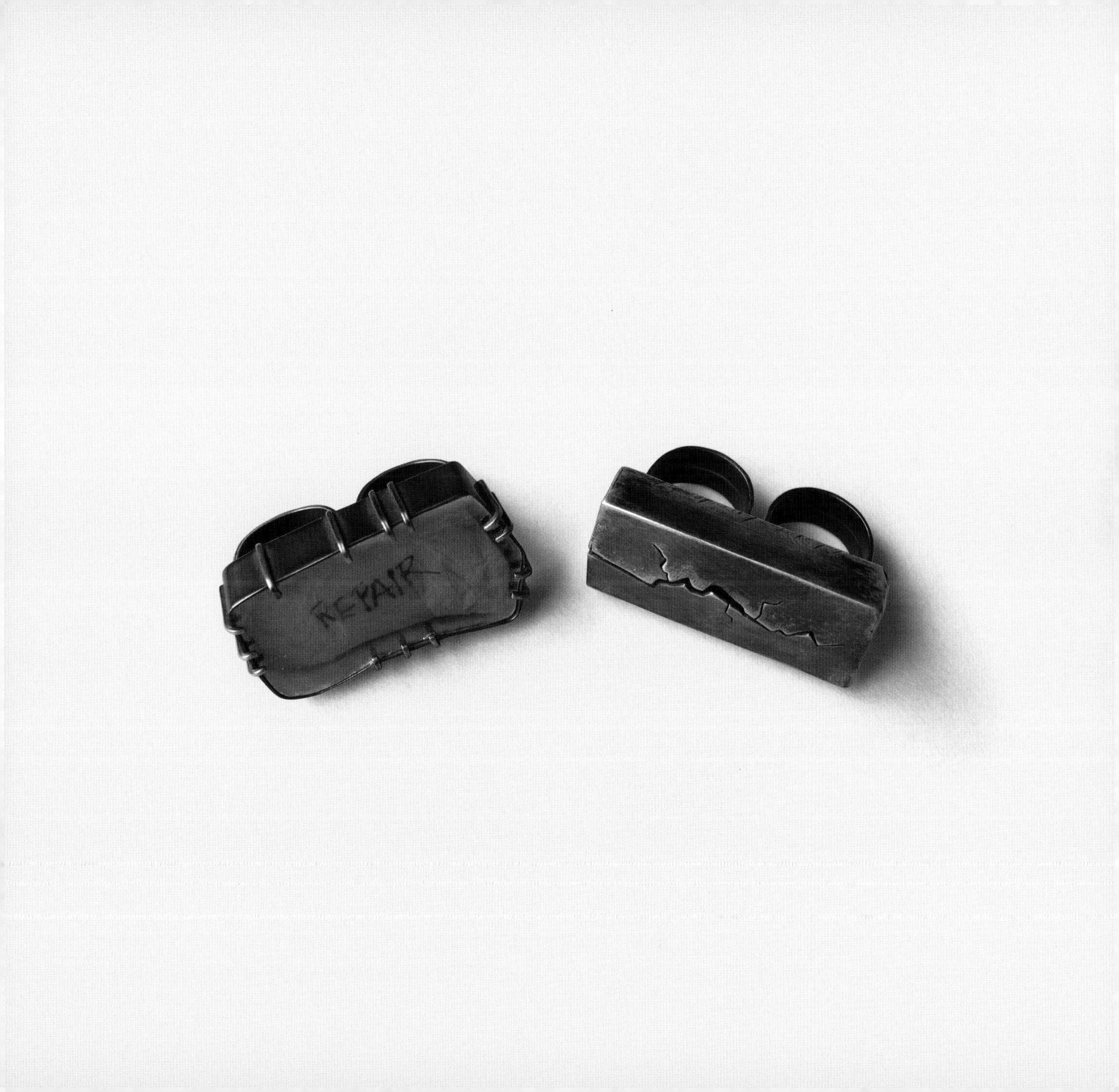
REPAIR

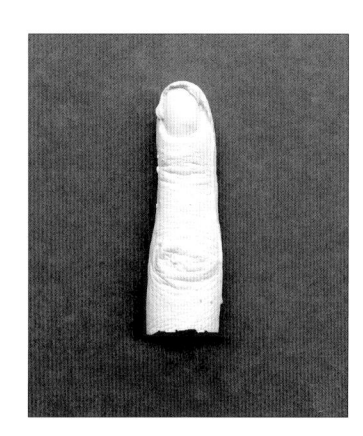

Lisa Gralnick

Kiff Slemmons
**Fingerlift**
Cart: 5 × 6 ½ × 1 ½
Finger Pendant: 3 × 1 × ½
Silver, cast plaster

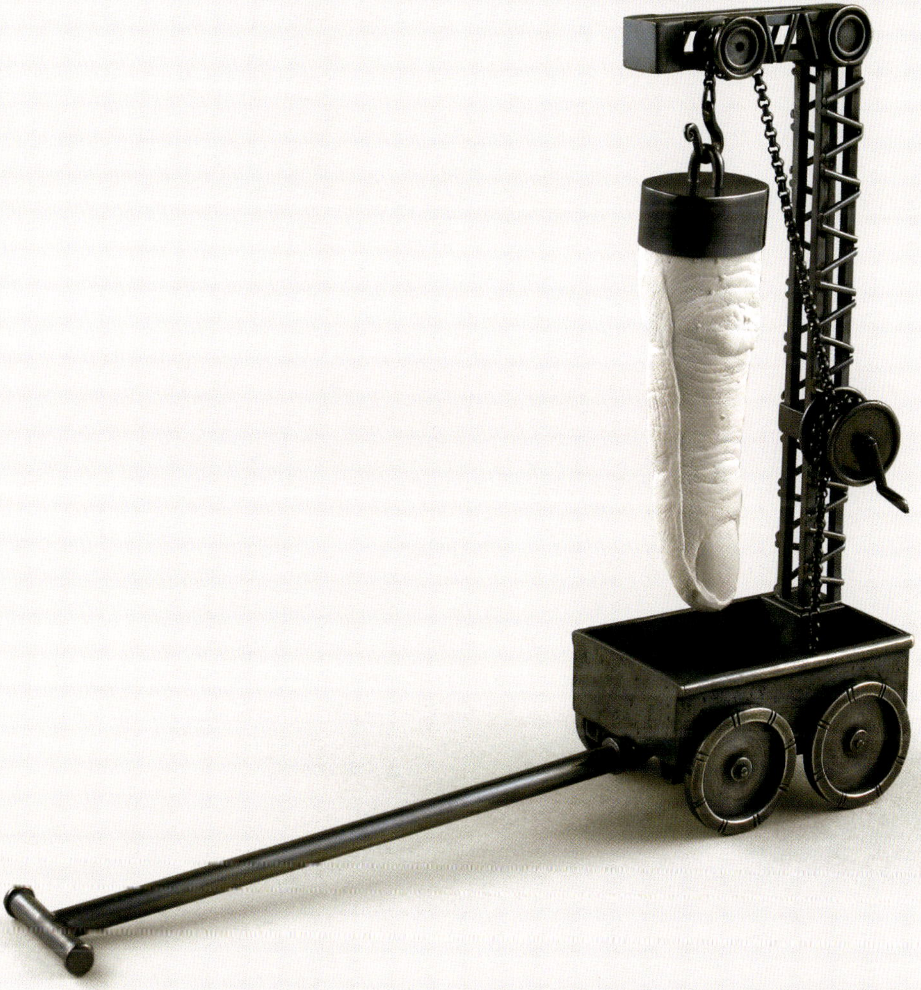

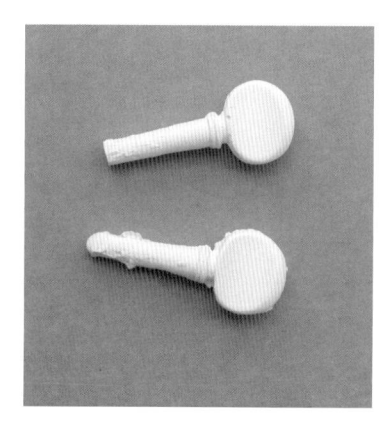

Lisa Gralnick

Kiff Slemmons
**Stopper**
Gun Pendant: 3¼ × 6 × ½
Ring: 1 × 2 × ⅛
Silver, cast plaster

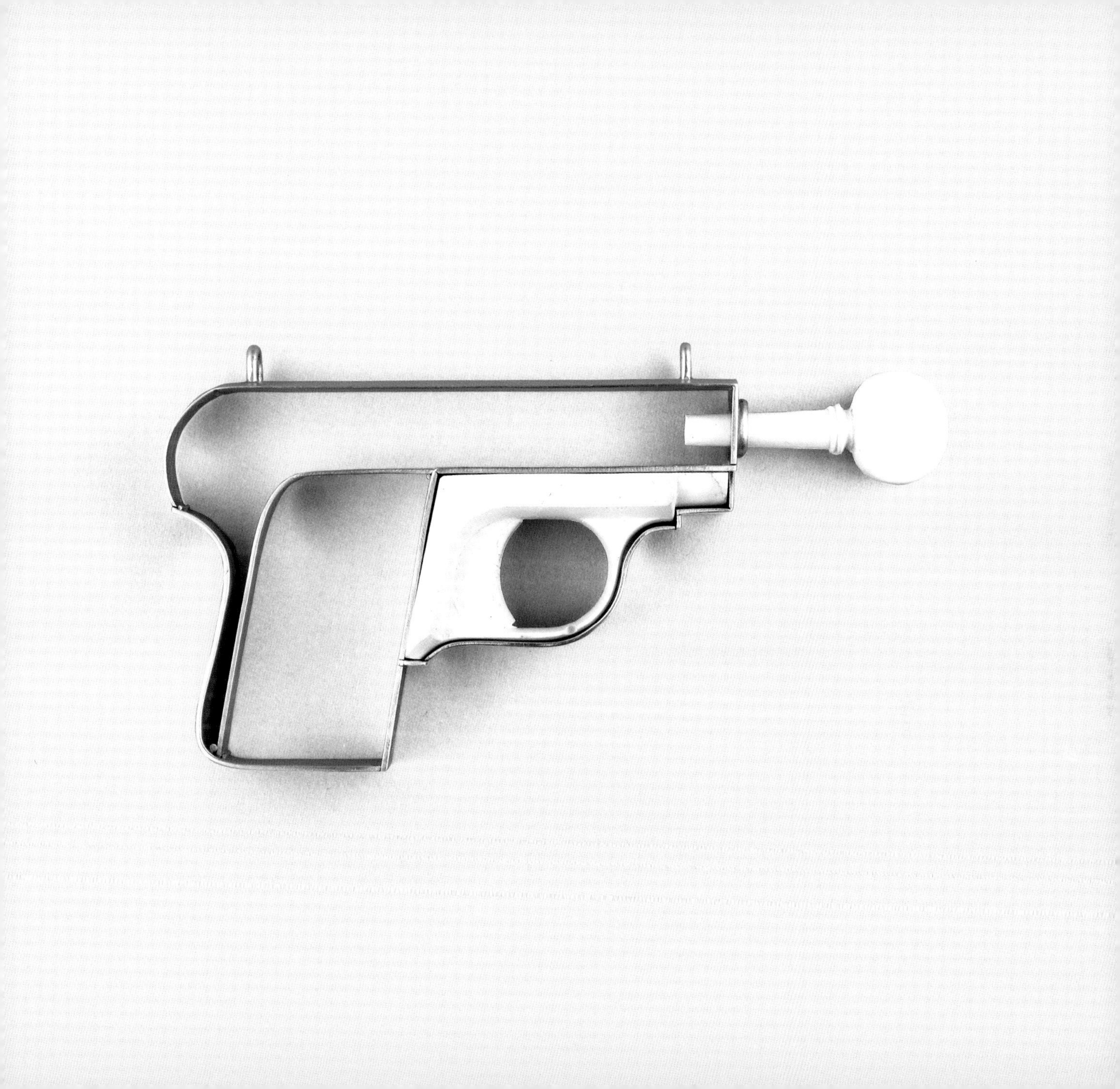

Gary Griffin

Kiff Slemmons
**Gridlock**
Pendant: 5¾ × 5¾ × 1
Steel, silver, street cleaner brush bristles

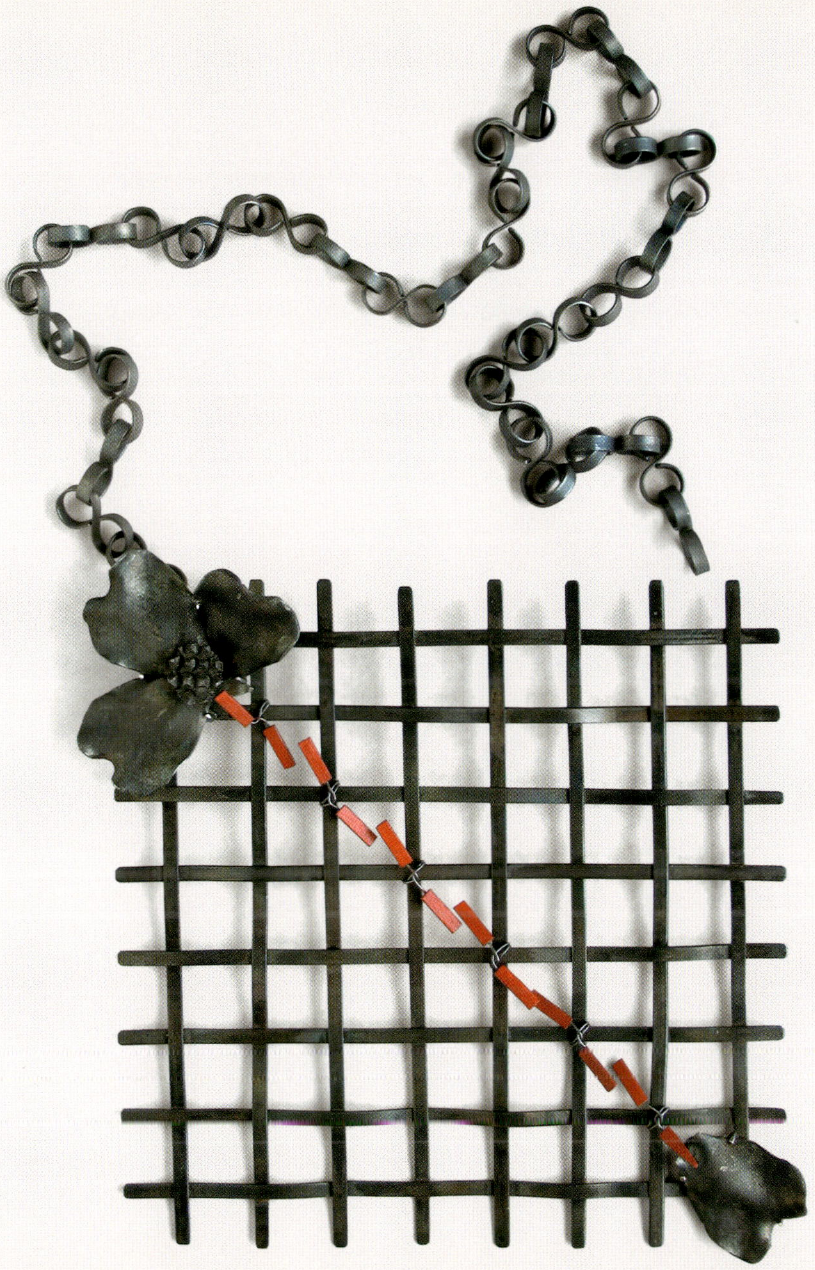

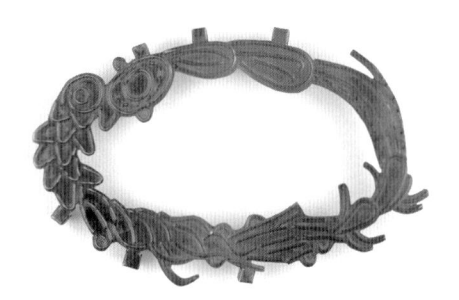

Esther Knobel

Kiff Slemmons
**Wreath**
Pin: 3 × 5 × ½
Brass, nickel silver, mica,
walrus whiskers,
Sanskrit fragment, paint

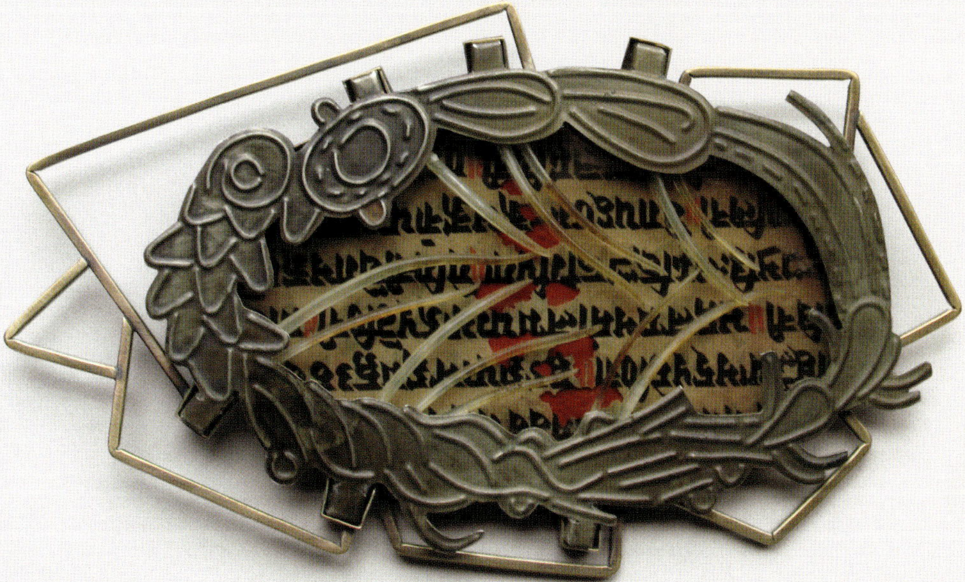

Esther Knobel

Kiff Slemmons
**Red Ink**
Pendant: 2 ¾ × 1 ½ × 1 ¼
Silver, nickel silver, paint

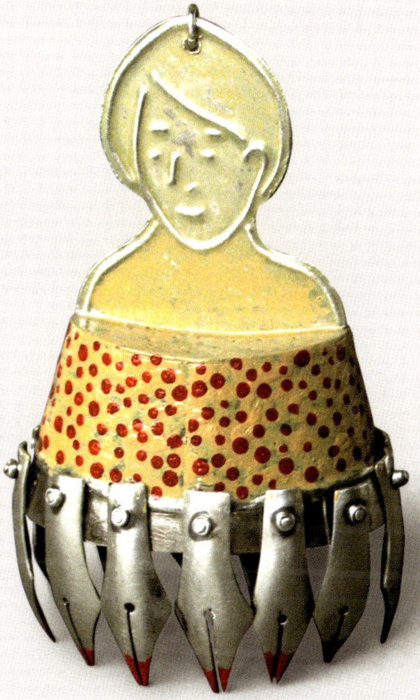

▶

Otto Künzli

Kiff Slemmons
**Rilke's Panther**
Toy/Necklace, 3 × 2½ × 1
Silver, rubber, gold

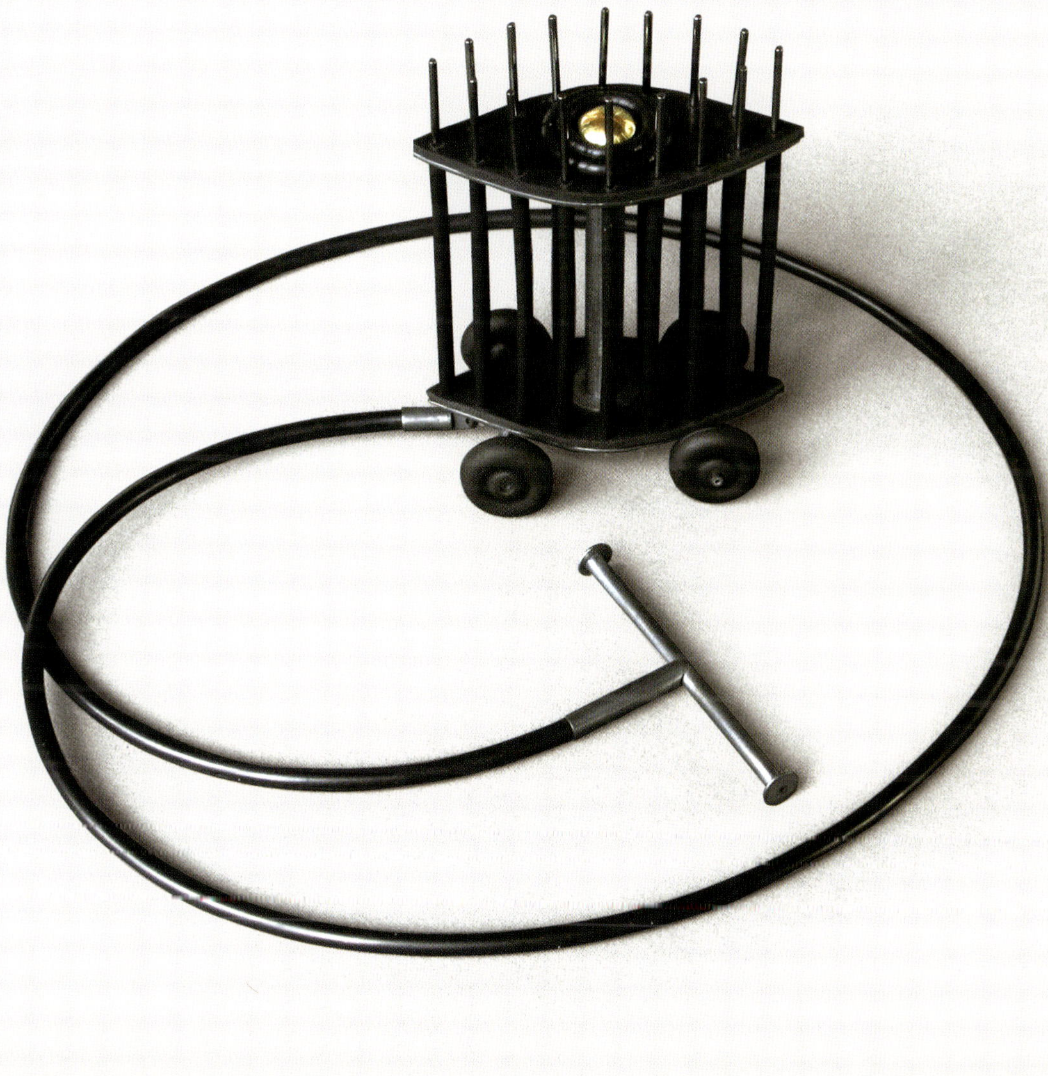

44 | 45

▶

Keith Lewis

Kiff Slemmons
**Lupanar Reliquary**
Pin: 7 ½ × 3 ½ × ½
Silver, dyed mother-of-pearl, amber, mica, fabric, wax

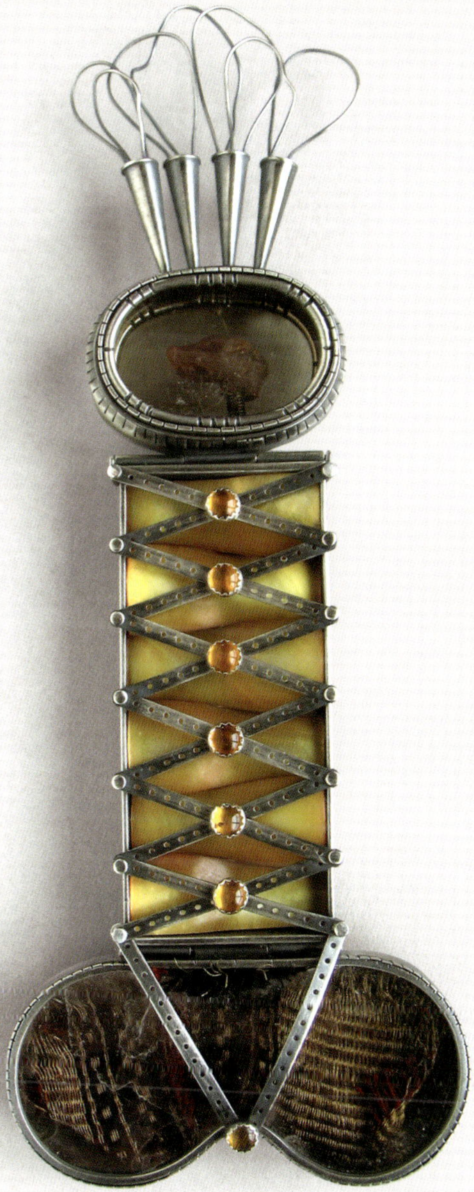

46 | 47

▶

Keith Lewis

Kiff Slemmons
**Osorio Lobo**
Pendant: 4¼ × 2½ × ¼
Silver, beeswax, mouse bones

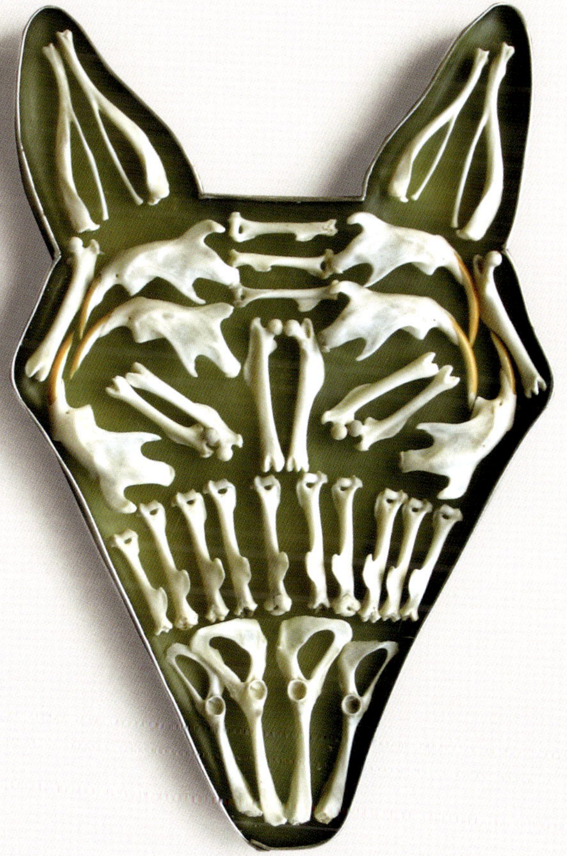

▶

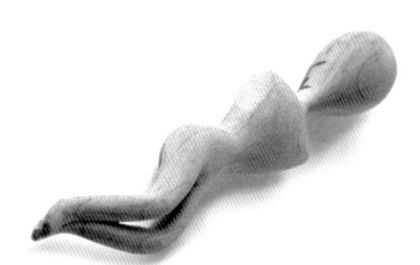

Bruce Metcalf

Kiff Slemmons
**Hot Bed**
Pin: 4¼ × 2½ × 1
Silver, carved wood, coral

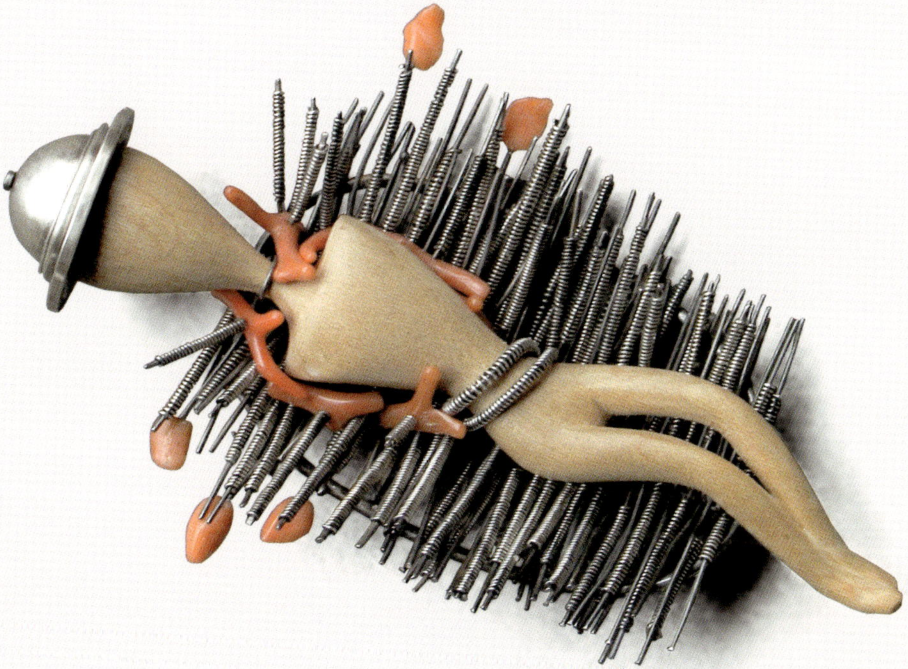

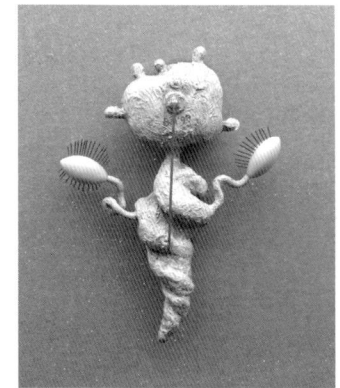

Bruce Metcalf

Kiff Slemmons
**Enunciation**
Frame: 11 × 8
Pin (figure): 4 × 3 × ¾
Silver, carved wood, plastic,
painted screw

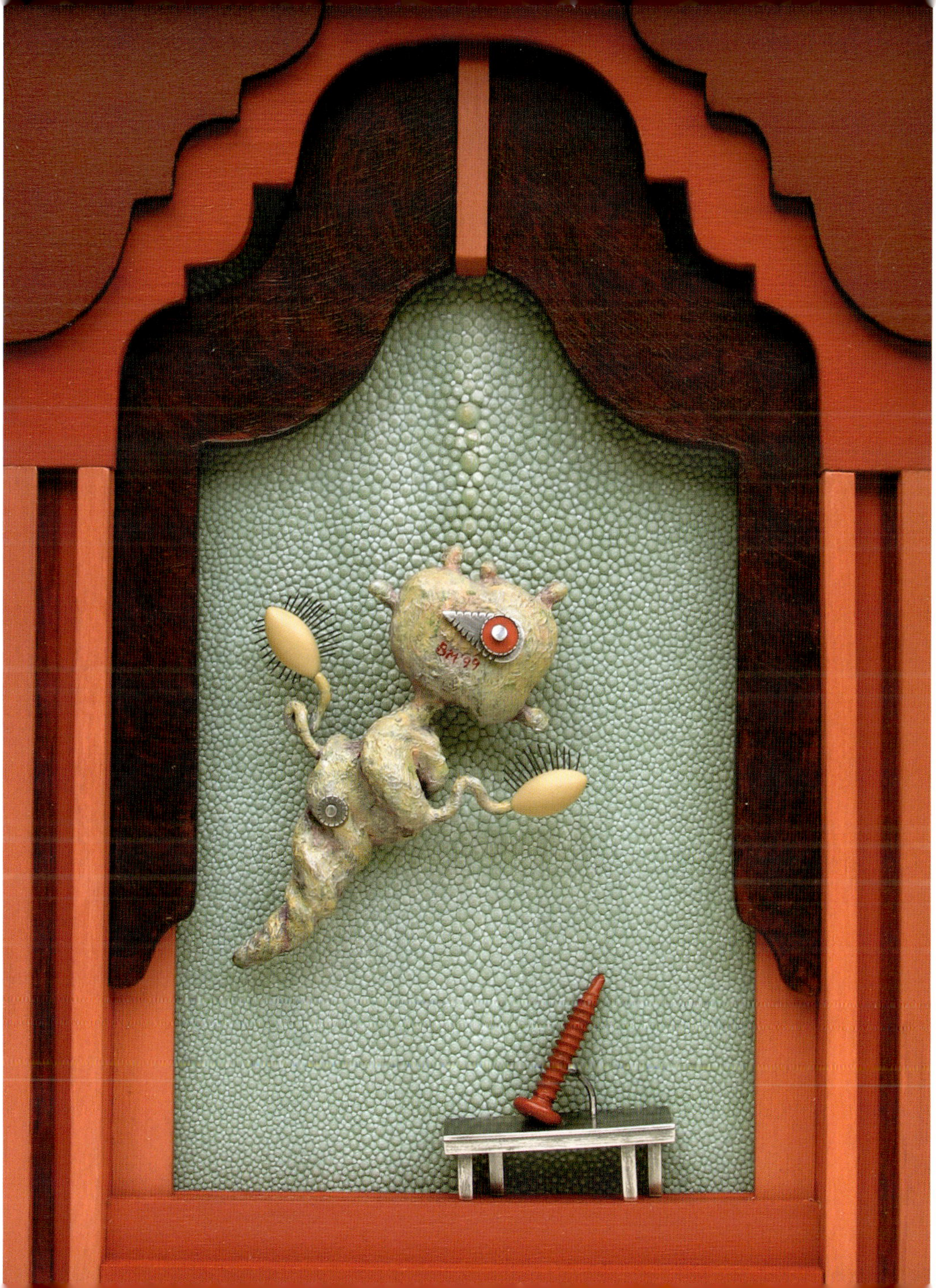

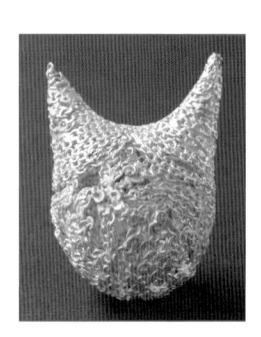

Myra Mimlitsch-Gray

Kiff Slemmons
**Bast**
Necklace: 3 ¾ × 2 ¼ × ¾
Silver

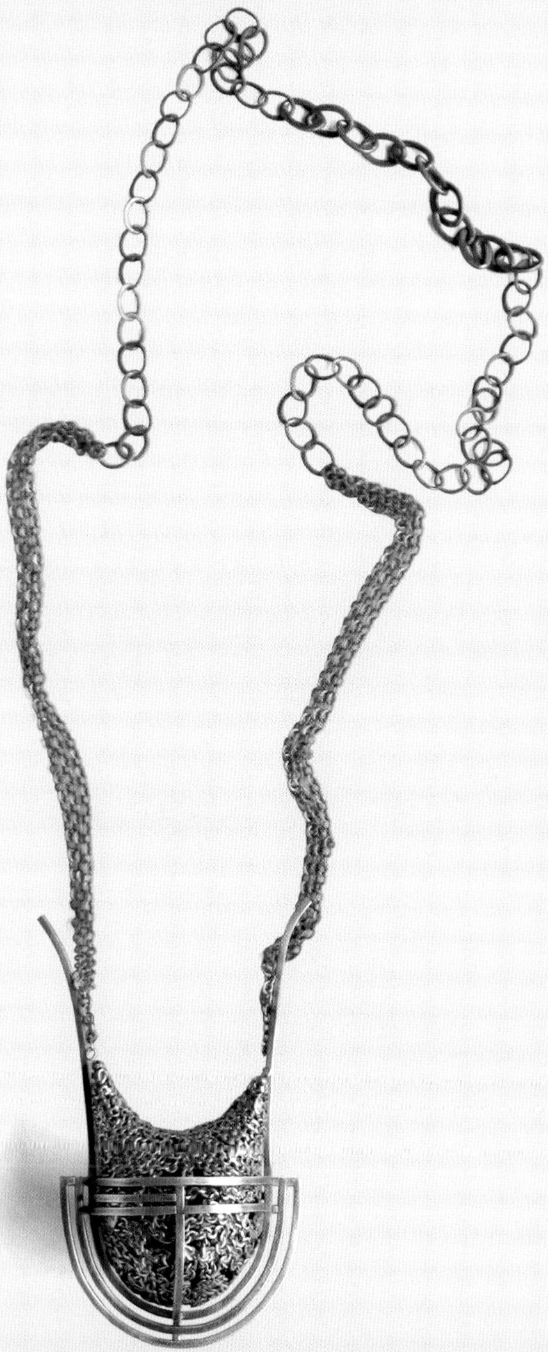

Daniel Jocz

Kiff Slemmons
**Warning**
Three pins together: 2 ½ × 8 × ¾
Silver, steel shell casings,
prismacolor

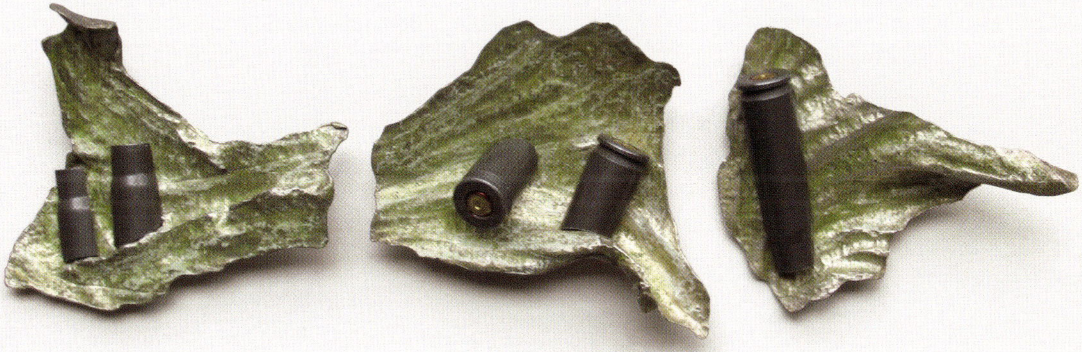

June Schwarcz

Kiff Slemmons
**Ember**
Pin: 1½ × 4½ × ½
Ebony, enameled copper

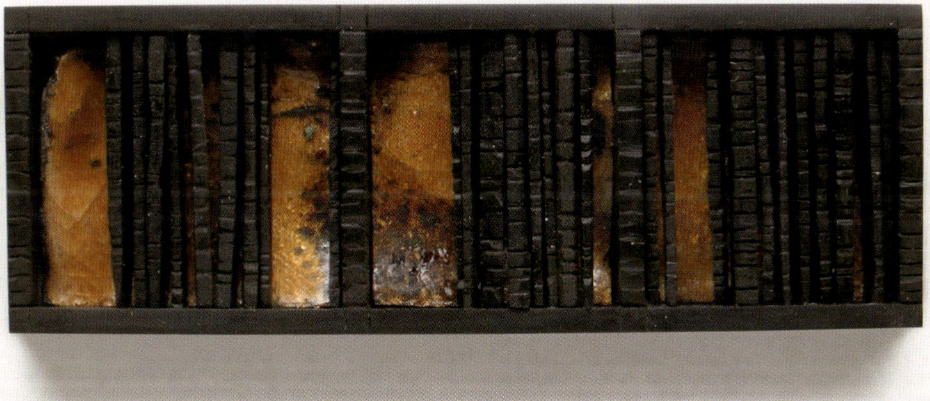

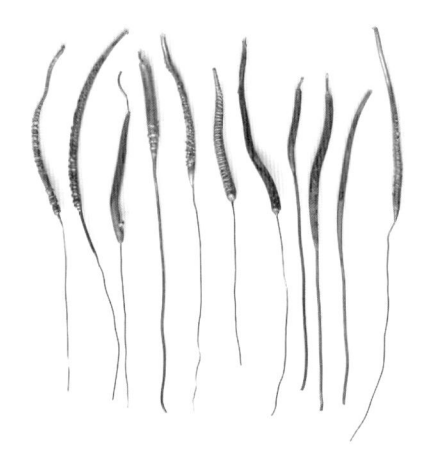

June Schwarcz

Kiff Slemmons
**Horn**
Pin: 1½ × 6 × ¾
Copper, enameled copper screen, silver

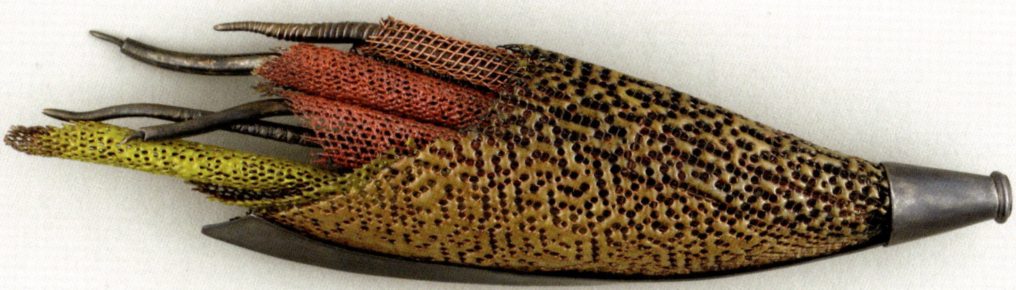

Joyce Scott

Kiff Slemmons
**Freed Speech**
Necklace: 14 × 10 × ½
Brass, mica, glass beads

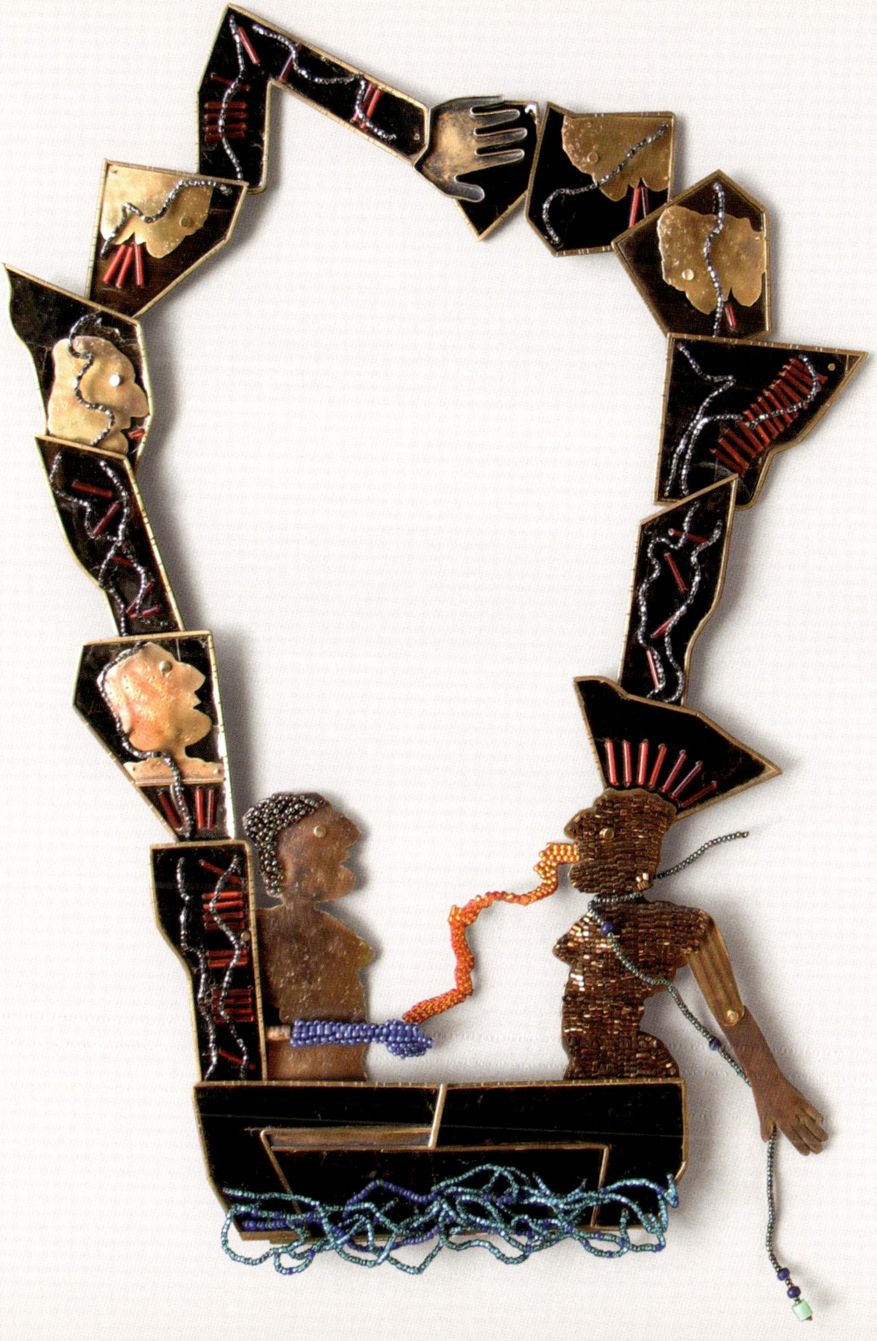

Ramona Solberg

Kiff Slemmons
**Monte Alban**
Pin: 3 × 2¾ × ½
Silver, clay replica

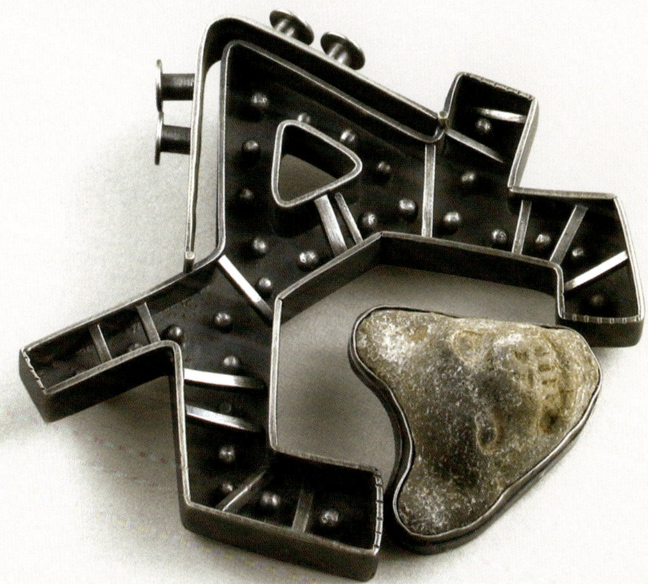

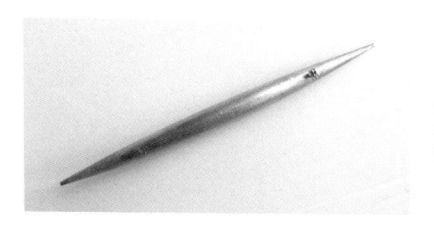

Rachelle Thiewes

Kiff Slemmons
▶ **Spray**
Two necklaces, 15 dia. × ½
Silver, handmade paper

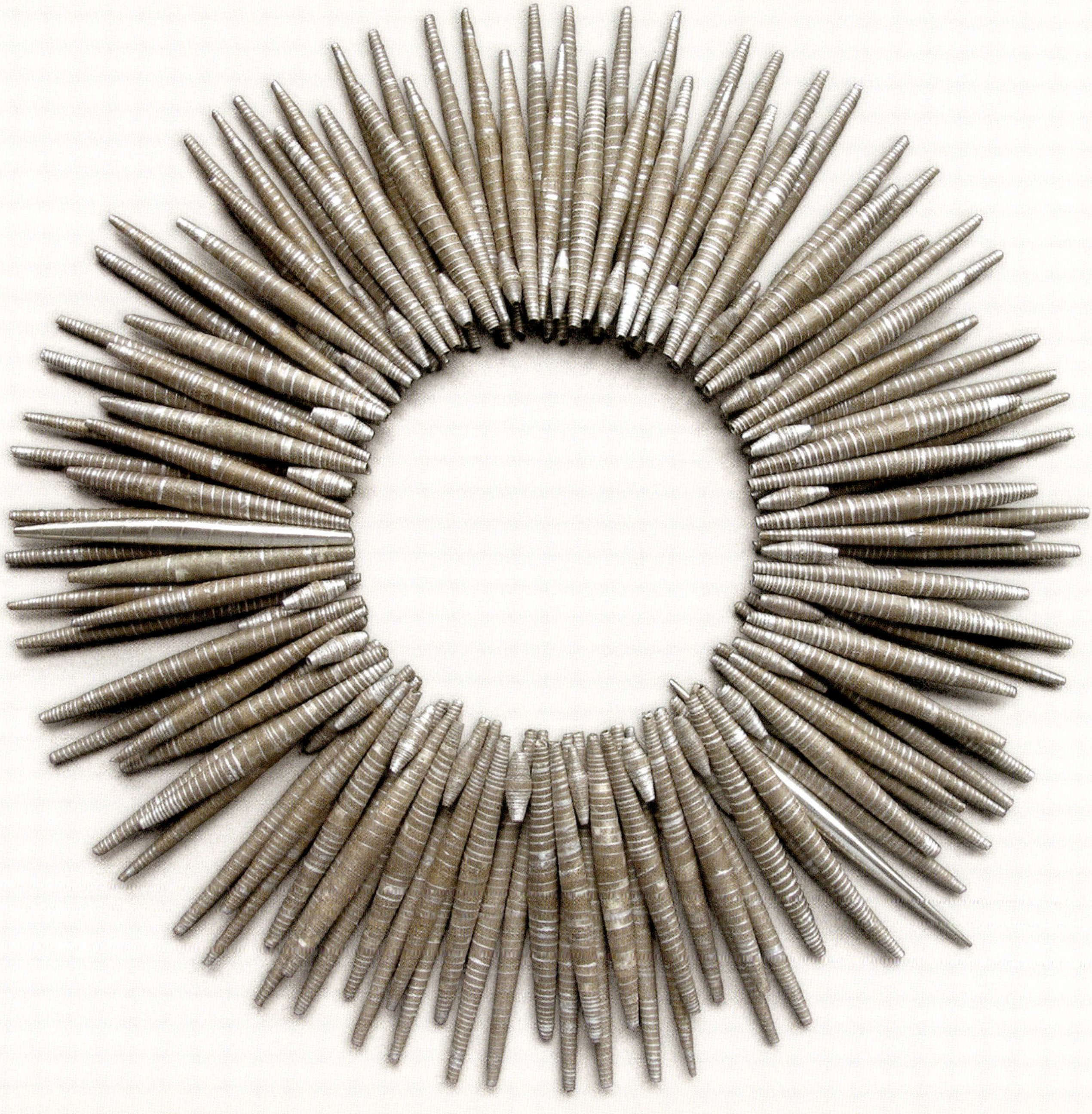

Terry Turrell

Kiff Slemmons
**Megaphone**
Ring: 2 × 2½ × 1½
Brass, painted fragment

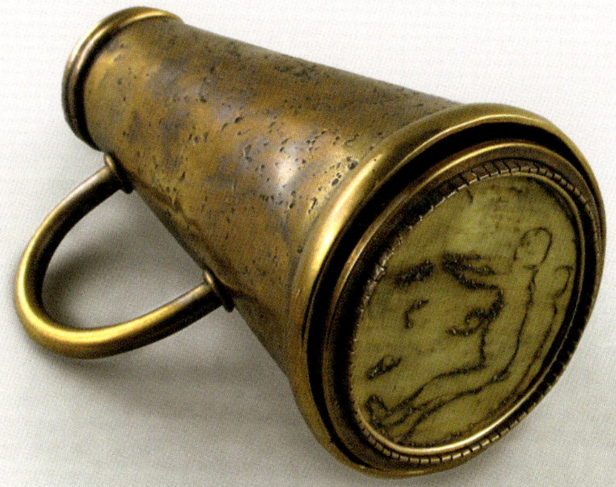

J. Fred Woell

Kiff Slemmons
**Caged Tulips**
Pin: 4 ¾ dia. × ½
Silver, glass filter, stamps,
2 CD's cut and painted, mica

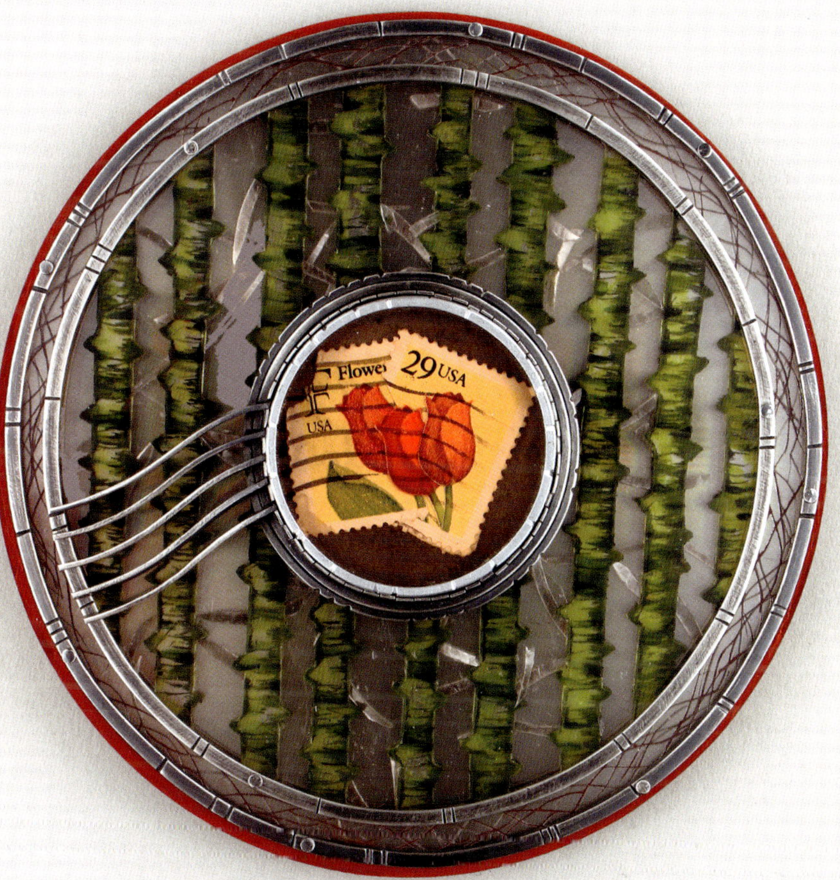
Flowe
29USA
USA

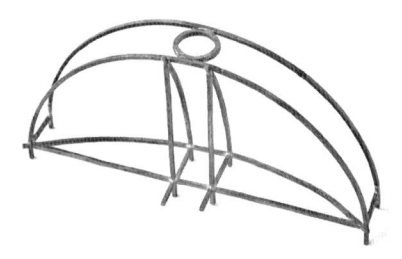

Joe Wood

Kiff Slemmons
**Two Points, One View**
Pin: 4 ½ × 10 × ¾
Silver, mica, paint

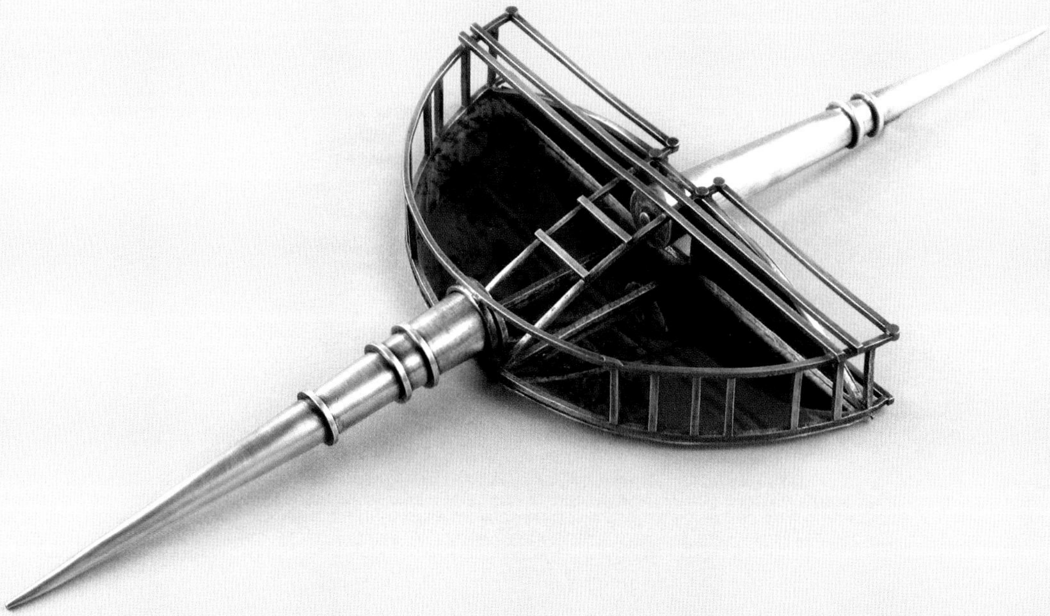

72 | 73

▶

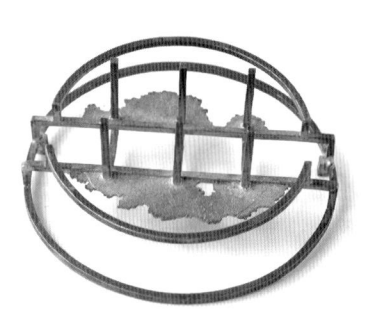

Joe Wood

Kiff Slemmons
**Bridge**
Pin: 3¼ dia. × 1
Silver, toy car, ebony

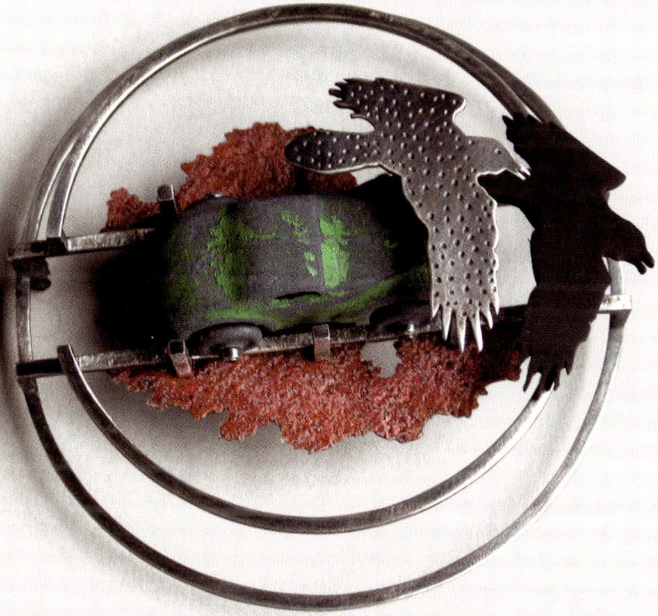

esteem the giver